Stars and Wishes

Gemma Owen-Kendall

BookLeaf Publishing

Presentation by *BookLeaf Publishing*

Web: www.bookleafpub.com

E-mail: info@bookleafpub.com

ISBN: 9789357210492

First edition 2022

To my special friend...

ACKNOWLEDGEMENT

I would like to express my special thanks to all the writers from my local area of North East Lincolnshire. You've all helped inspire me to write my first ever poetry collection.

PREFACE

Thank you for giving the chance to read my first ever collection of poems. Poetry isn't something I usually write but in recent years, I've had a lot of feelings to express so I've put these into poems.

One Day I Will.

One day I will hold your hand and never let go.

One day I will hold you, forever and now.

One day I will be your girl but until then,

I will wait for that one day when we can be
whole.

I Never Knew

I never knew love existed until I met you.
The feeling of never wanting you out of my life.

I never knew love existed until I kissed you. The feeling of never wanting to stop kissing you.

I never knew love existed until you told me, you loved me first. The feeling of never wanting to stop loving you torments me.

I never knew love until you showed me how to love you. The feeling of wanting this with you forever and always.

Love, That Feeling

Love, that feeling of wanting to share a life with another.

Love, of knowing it is you I want to be with.

Love, to me is more than just a word.

Love, just wanting to share my emotions with you.

Love, that feeling of wanting to take a risk.

Love, to want it and always have it.

I Only Wish

I only wish to see you once again, to have those dreamy eyes gazing back into mine.

I only wish to stroke my hands through your hair and kiss those luscious lips of yours.

I only wish to know what fate has lined up for us, but I guess I will never know.

I only wish to wonder if I ever cross your mind, your thoughts or if you've forgotten all about me.

I only wish upon a falling star to see you once again.

I only wish when I blew the candle out on my birthday cake to see and speak to you again.

I only wish to just run up to you and wrap my arms around you like nothing ever happened.

I only wish to miss you deeply as you will always have a place in my heart.

Those months we shared were enough to love a lifetime's worth, I only wish to have all this again with you.   5

I'm on a Journey

I'm on a journey to discover and find myself once again but not the type of travel to go to a new place.

I'm on a journey to be at peace with my emotions on the day heartbreak is caused by you. The continous feels of anxiety and chest pain have slowly eased, they're at bay.

I'm on a journey to forgive you but I know I will never get over you. As you will always have a special place in my heart that I intend to hold dear.

I'm on a journey to be me once again, but I wish for what we had to have never ended. I was and still am so fragile minded to come to grips with what love truly is.

A Shooting Star

That evening, I took a drive in my car,
I glanced up at the starry night sky.

There is was before my eyes, a shooting star
right there before me but from afar.

The saying is to wish upon a star, if only I could
catch it in a jar.

The one thing I do want to wish for, is to have
my heart with you.

Quest For Love

Life is sacred and beautiful specially to have you in it, before we spoke I was a lost soul and losing sight of who I was as a person.

I've always had this idea about what love is truly like and how it should be, but it's never been there for me. I've been searching for that one person who can whisk me off my feet, take me on a journey of love as well as save me from losing myself.

I believe and know that person is you, it's as though the fates have bought us together and now, I don't want to lose sight of you. Without knowing, I have written many stories about you and never realised you would be crafted into a real person. I've longed to have a guy who is dark and mysterious, as well as sexy and good looking, now you are finally here and I hope you will be the hero of my story on my quest to find love and myself again.

From The Very First Moment

From the very first moment that I saw you, I was
always intrigued by you.

From the very first moment that I saw you, I
obviously had some hidden desire for you.

From the very first moment that we finally
spoke, I never knew how much of an impact I
had on you.

From the very first moment that I'd dreamed of
you, my hidden desire of you erupted.

From the very first moment that our friendship
blossomed, I knew I longed to belong to you.

Starry Night Sky

Oh starry night sky, twinkling above me,
sparkling upon this night sky.

Oh starry night sky, please grant me my wishes
upon this sparkling night sky.

Oh starry night sky with your dazzling lights,
burning above me upon this nightly lit sky.

Please watch over me as you twinkle above me
on this starry night sky.

I Remember

I remember the first time we met, I couldn't take my eyes off of you.

I remember the first time we spoke, I couldn't get you off my mind.

I remember the first time we kissed, that magical moment I will never forget.

I remember the first time you told me you loved me, this is a memory I hold dear.

I remember all my first times with you, I remember them all too well and will never forget these moments.

Is This Goodbye?

12

Is this goodbye? I hope it's only for now and not forever. I'm struggling to keep my feelings at bay.

Is this goodbye? I hope it's not for good. I'm struggling to come to terms with you not being here today.

Is this goodbye? I hope this is not for real. I'm struggling to accept I may have been led astray.

Is this goodbye? Oh please I hope it is not. I'm struggling to be okay as each day passes by.

My Heart

My heart is not just an organ, a muscle, or a
vessel to pump blood through my arteries around
my body.

My heart feels my thoughts and emotions, it
knows what it wants.

My heart is not just a part of my body fulfilling
its daily duties.

My heart feels my strengths and weaknesses, it
takes over my soul. It is part of my soul.

My heart loves and breaks easily, the heart can't
help who it chooses to belong to.

My heart chooses to belong to you, my love.

Crush

How can some small crush transpire into
something more? From just gazing at you to a
rush of fluttering butterflies in my tummy.

How can some small crush spiral into a dream
about you? I'm just so crazy about you, wanting
to have more from you.

How can some small crush fire up into a love
whirl with you? You fulfilled my every desire
leaving me to crave more of you.

The Mask

Why do you hide behind a persona of pretending
to be someone or something else. It's as though
you are wearing a mask.

Why do you hide away from me and yet watch
over me from a distance. It's as though you want
to be my hero but you just hold back.

Why do you hide behind a camouflage mask, the
soft green cloth covering the lower part of your
face. It's as though you are some stow away.

Why do you hide away from me your true self,
does the real you ever exist or is it concealed at
bay.

Why do you hide behind your nickname, Ninja.
It's as though you always see yourself behind the
mask of one.

I Miss You

I miss you so much, like the sky needs the sun.

I miss you so much, like the trees need the
leaves.

I miss you so much, like the night sky needs the
stars.

I miss you so much, like the flowers need petals.

I miss you so much, like the Earth needs the
oceans.

I miss you so very much, just like my heart
needs you.

Teenage Dream

To live those moments once again of feeling younger, like a teenager. Not having a care in the world until I saw you. To lock eyes with you and not wanting to look away. Reliving those moments again of first love and innocence, just like a teenager. Even more so it's that you're feeling this moment like me. It is as though we are reliving our teenage dreams once again. Sneaking out and meeting up in secluded places where we can't be seen by prying eyes. I hope we can have another teenage dream one day, to have the first hand touch to the first kiss.

I Hate You, I Love You

I hate you, I hate what you've done to me, you've crushed me you b***ard and now you must pay the price. Over and over in my head I hear you telling me how much you loved me but it was all lies. I let you get into my head and I let you get into my body and now you've just vanished without a trace. Did I ever mean anything to you? I did so much for you, I was prepared to change my entire life to be with you but you asked me to wait. Well I did wait and now you've just disappeared.

Some days I imagine finding you and stabbing you over and over again so you can feel how much you've made me suffer. Every puncture from the blade piercing your heart bit by bit. Blood splattering out as I continue to break your heart like you did with mine. Other days I fantasise about us meeting up again and having make up hugs, feeling your touch once again and kissing those luscious lips of yours. But I can't hurt you like you have me as it's not in my nature. I still love you and as much as it hurts, I will no doubt forgive you.

Missing You

It pains me to write this to you but I have to get this off my chest. It's been nearly a year since I last saw you and we last spoke together. We used to talk, text and phone each other everyday but now we don't talk anymore. You haven't phoned or responded to the couple of messages that I've sent to you. What did I do to deserve this? What did I do for you to suddenly not acknowledge my existence anymore? I was there for you when you wanted to chat and get things off your chest. I was there for you when you needed money and I was there for you when you felt down.

I still remember everything you told me, that you fell in love with me and that you wanted to be with me. I still remember all the secrets you shared with me and I promised not to tell anyone. I still remember you constantly telling me that you love me all the stars in the sky and more, that you wished, hoped and prayed for one day for us to be together.

You told me that I had a big heart and a lot of love to give. You told me that you had never met anyone like me before. You told me that I was your special girl. You told me that you hoped one day to marry me. You told me always and forever, you and me against the world.

Was I stupid enough to believe you? Yes I believed everything you said and still do. I don't know why but I do. I miss you even when I used to see you everyday. I miss you like the sky misses the sun on a rainy day. I miss yo, do you miss me too?

I hate that you've broken me, I hate that you've broken my heart. I hate that I don't you and I hate that I don't get to talk to you. I truly hope one day you will come back into my life again. As I hate feeling so broken and I hate missing you so much. Wherever you are and whatever you are doing, know that I still love you. Please come back to me.

www.ingramcontent.com/pod-product-compliance
Lightning Source LLC
LaVergne TN
LVHW021719210726

843509LV00021B/2821